MW01223628

ARE YOU IN THERE?

Conny (Whittaker) Saunders

 **FriesenPress**

Suite 300 - 990 Fort St
Victoria, BC, Canada, V8V 3K2
www.friesenpress.com

Copyright © 2015 by Conny (Whittaker) Saunders
First Edition — 2015

All rights reserved.

No part of this publication may be reproduced in any form, or
by any means, electronic or mechanical, including photocopying,
recording, or any information browsing, storage, or retrieval
system, without permission in writing from the publisher.

ISBN
978-1-4602-7011-0 (Hardcover)
978-1-4602-7012-7 (Paperback)
978-1-4602-7013-4 (eBook)

1. Biography & Autobiography, Personal Memoirs

Distributed to the trade by The Ingram Book Company

Table of Contents

Having received my GED diploma on June 3, 2013 at the age of 56, I feel honoured and proud to have accomplished the achievement. Now publishing a book, I am quite overwhelmed. It is a true fact that no matter what age you are, you can achieve goals. I spent my life travelling in the Maritimes and throughout the West Coast of Canada, And currently reside in New Brunswick.

Dedication

I dedicate this book to my significant other.

He is my companion, my love, and best friend.

He will always hold the key to my heart.

Also to my family and friends, who have
helped me through this journey.

A special dedication in memory of family
and friends who have passed on.

Their thoughts and Inspiration carried me through life,

To be the writer that I am.

A Change Within Yourself

As you go through life questioning your motives
about how you want to make a change within yourself
you will know and feel when the time is right.
Your mind will race a mile a minute.
It will try to nurture you
into making the right choices.
Your heart will feel the vibration
of longing for a change.
Feel what your heart is feeling;
exert yourself to the fullest.
Your spiritual soul is the deepest part of you.
It is up to you to have faith.
Rest assured, changes do not happen
in the blink of an eye.
You will search for answers to where your security lies
but this will dissolve in time.
Procrastinating to overcome any obstacle
that has blocked your achievements
is your soul's responsibility.
Choose wisely the changes you are about to make.
Remember that you and only you
have the power to change yourself.

A Feast to Remember

At the crack of dawn, I watched the sunrise.
The bright red yellow sky
Brought a sparkle to my eye.
There over yonder stood a lumberjack guy.
He was chopping wood as hard as he could,
sweat pouring off his chest.
Is he single? Should I dare to guess?
It's time to have a Thanksgiving feast.
My mind tells me to invite the manly beast.
Out of my log cabin, I strolled over to his R.V.
Oh my, is he staring at me?
Pray tell me he's single and free.
''Good day" to you Mr. Lumberjack guy.
He turned away as if he were shy.
I invited him and the missus over
for a Thanksgiving feast.
"I'm single" he replied. What a relief!
His closeness I felt as I set the table for two.
The turkey I prepared was blessed for me and you.

A Writer Within

I will leave you alone for a week or so
I am not on schedule, you need to know.
My writing is spontaneous,
I strive to be a creative genius.
Patience is a virtue,
I gather my thoughts
At a steady pace.
I'm keeping you, as reader, truly amazed.
I feel the need
To assure you I exist.
Now release your imaginary mind,
search for the writer
who's been toying with you
For quite some time.
I guess that's why I am known
as the writer within.

All My Children

My children, my grandchildren, my great-grandchildren,
it's so nice of you to visit me.
How thoughtful of you not to forget about me.
Are these your pictures hanging on the wall?
Yes those are our pictures.
Can you tell me who's who? Refresh my memory.
How does one think of me and you?
She's forgotten that we've all grown up.
Come on now my children,
please take me out for a walk, listen to me as I talk.
With a little help from us, we assured her
That we were all grown up.
Her laughter, love and joy keep her memories
from fading away.
She knows in her heart we will be there everyday.
Do you have a fear of coming to see me?
If so give me a chance to set those worries free.
My children, my grandchildren, my great-grandchildren,
please forgive me as my memory fails me.
All I remember is that you all belong to me.

At A Distance

At a distance I watched you
As you saddled up your horse.
Catching a glimpse of you,
I yearned with desire to join you.
Control I had, yet my heart
Was telling me to explore.
At a distance I saddled up my horse,
picturing you and me,
our hearts on fire.
Side by side we would gallop
along the ocean shore.
The passion we felt would inspire us
to go the distance, to chase a dream,
to imagine beyond our control
the wildest thing.
At a distance we dismount.
Catching a glimpse of each other
we could not fight the feeling any longer.
Walking to greet, our hearts felt the desire,
the passion; the cost of true love
Could only be admired.

Bar Room Brawl

You start a bar room brawl.
You stagger down the hall.
Your anger gets the better of you,
now it's your call
to end this bar room brawl.
You're out of control.
You smash a bottle
over your opponent's head.
He falls to the ground.
You're scared,
you're thinking he's dead.
He comes around,
he begs you to let him go.
Cops arrive on the scene.
Witnesses denied
having seen anything.
My opponent was too weak
He could not speak.
I had to come clean.
Spending time behind prison walls,
a voice within kept hollering,
"It's your call.
Only you can put an end
to the haunting memories
of the bar room brawl."

Burning Bridges

I came to my senses, my body trembling.
Helplessly, I watched the burning bridge
collapse to the ground.
Everything ablaze, everything astounding.
The fiery blaze was contained by massive rain.
Flying into a total rage I felt almost insane
and stood there like a total fool.
How could I have let my heart rule?
The foundation of the burning bridge turns to coal.
It's time to let go of my broken heart and soul.
The bridge of love is no longer there,
I will not linger in despair.
Burning bridges tumble to the ground,
a new foundation of love must be found.

Butt Out

The war is on, our nerves are gone.
The smoking habit went far beyond.
We tried to quit many times before
Never succeeding; always the urge
To have one more.

The older you get, the harder it is.
We thought quitting smoking would be a whiz.
You choke you, croak, go ahead, have another smoke.
When you're on your way out, don't forget to butt out.

Roses of Yesteryear

The roses of yesteryear are still on my mind,
not able to remember whether they were yellow or red.
A yellow rose represented a friendship
we vowed never to let go.
A red rose, we felt the bond,
but now our lives have changed.
Yet the roses of yesteryear still linger in my mind.
I feel the urge to hold you,
to be near to you.
Could we not have changed the colour of the rose?
It was Valentine's Day and Cupid was searching
for two hearts to bond.
How he found us I cannot recall.
Both hearts were spoken for at the time.
The roses of yesteryear still linger in my mind.
We sacrifice the feelings of what we had back then
brought together for a moment of truth.
It was then we realized that we were the best of friends.
May the memory of the roses of yesteryear never end.

Cheaters

A cheater they say never gains, only feels their self-righteous pain.
Grieving with sorrow, swearing never again.
Misery of self, addiction that seldom ends,
if only they would realize it takes time to
make amends.
As a cheater pleads for mercy,
for you to open your heart,
their counting on you for a fresh new start.
Making mistakes we sometimes regret.
Cheaters are human, lest we forget
to allow a cheater to erase their mistakes.
Love conquers all; one must have faith.

Chickens, Feathers, Rainbow of Gold

Some say you will see the rainbow of gold.
Do you not realize I am growing old?
Chickens today, feathers tomorrow –
in this saying lies my joy and sorrow.
My pay check is the chicken
in the palm of my hand.
But mere feathers are left
when the pay check is gone.
The rainbow of gold I am yet to see,
oh my lord have mercy on me.
Feathers cling to what's left of my pay
as I struggle to save for that rainy day.
My rainbow of gold I now realize
is not chickens or feathers –
it's the will to survive.

Ching Ching

Ching ching was the sound of the slot machine.
Pray tell me, my love, where are our wedding rings?
I see the look of betrayal in his eyes
and I pray it's untrue as he utters a sigh.
He speaks to me in a dark harsh voice
"My dear, you have gone and left me no choice."
Turning his head towards the loud ching ching:
"There lies your answer about our rings."
I know the slots have swallowed our rings.
I reach out my hand to stop his scheme.
I wake up to realize it was only a dream.

Christmas Card

'Twas the spirit of Christmas and New Year coming upon us
I searched high and low for that special Christmas card.
Each card I read, thinking for one moment
that I could hear a voice within,
but that voice did not reply.

A voice within that card should tell us to open our eyes,
to fill our hearts with joy and to give praise
to loved ones that are far and near.
Take a moment to rejoice
as we say goodbye to another year.

Take a cup of kindness as you gather with family and friends
at the strike of midnight
to sing the song of Auld Lang Syne.
Merry Christmas to all and a Happy New Year
from my family to yours.

Country Home

Taking a stroll down memory lane,
wondering if the old house still looks the same.
I recall the aroma of freshly baked bread and pies –
how it always kept your heart so memorized.
I still hear the crackling sound
of wood burning in the fireplace.
I wonder if our pictures
are still hung over the mantelpiece.
Wait! What about the two rocking chairs
that were on the front porch?
How the years have gone by,
still hanging on to the love torch.
As the door opened, I walked in.
A young couple stood there arm-in-arm.
"Please come in, let your story begin."
"This was our country home long ago.

The two rocking chairs where did they go?"
"We placed them in front of the fireplace.
We kept your pictures, there, hung over the mantelpiece."
"I must be boring you by now." They smiled at me.
"Would you like to see your kitchen now?" "Yes, please!"
There was no smell of bread or a pie being baked.
"There must be some mistake. Am I in the right kitchen?"
"That you are, dear," putting an apron around me.

Now let the baking begin.
The aroma of the freshly baked bread and pies
Will always keep your heart memorized.
It was time to say goodbye to our country home.
The young couple that we now know,
have blended their love
into the savour of our home.

Controlled Love

My love, you mastered the art
of jealously and control.
Your cowardly ways
put our love on hold.
Resenting sleepless nights,
I pray everything will be all right.
The tone of your voice
leaves me quivering with fright.
Desperately trying to believe in you,
forgiving you, in the moment of truth.
Jealously, control, your obsession,
drives me into a deep depression.
Shall I grieve your envious ways?
Or become the devious one
to make your heart sway.

Staring closely
into his deceiving eyes
was I listening to a pack of lies?
He bowed his head in deepest shame,
realizing he was the one to blame.
"Mercy," he pleaded again and again.
"Help me stop my controlling game."

Cry Wolf

The howling wolf close to my heels,
running rapidly into the hills.
Not a moment to catch my breath
nor to stand still,
the wolf still on my heels.
The cabin was close but I could not stop,
the cunning wolf was too sly.
He let out a howl, you must not cry.
"Come here," he said. "Stand by me,
admit to yourself you cannot hide.
Give people a chance to believe in you.
Prove to yourself that you can speak the truth."
Crying the blues, pretending to fake sick,
He knew I was up to my old tricks.
"Why," he said, "are you so deceitful?
Do you not care how much you hurt other people?"
His judgment of me was too keen.
"You don't know me; I'm not that mean."
He vanished out of sight,
leaving me in a terrible fright.
I looked around, he was nowhere to be seen.
Arriving at the cabin I opened the door.
There was the wolf dead on the floor.
I kneeled down beside him to pat his head,
I put my arms around him.
"Please forgive me and all my sins,
help me to open up my heart,
let my new life begin.
I swear to you I'll never cry wolf again."

Devotion

The sixty-seven metallic green mustang –
after thirty-five years it's still part of the scene.
Cruisin' down country roads mile after mile –
now the story must be told.
I courted you in old-fashioned style,
In July of seventy-two.
The loyalty, the feeling of devotion,
as we became one.
It's seems like only yesterday
that our marriage had just begun.
Now fulfilling the role of parents and grandparents
with the old mustang still in our hearts.
It will cruise with us from here to eternity,
devoted we are to become one.

Don't Tempt Me

Don't tempt me with the sweet taste
of wine upon my lips!
The fragrance of your cologne
that I used to smell.
To touch you, to hold you, in the moment
of passion, I can only prevail.

Don't tempt me as we drive
through the covered wooden bridge!
Stopping in the centre,
face-to-face, so tempted,
so close, to feel the love of yesterday.
Our signatures were carved inside the covered bridge.

Don't tempt me to want those feelings of yesterday!
The kiss, holding your hand –
it wasn't a dream, it was reality.
The bond between us
brought forth from the love of yesterday.

Driftwood

Walking barefoot along the ocean shore
Seeing the driftwood coming afloat
A piece of wood that comes and goes,
not knowing the direction it will flow
with the call of the ocean, it stays afloat.
Further I walk along the shore
still with the driftwood
all shattered and scorched.
Should I set it adrift or consider its ways?
What would it say?
What if it could talk?
What if it could feel?
What if it were real?
Wherever the driftwood floats ashore
it calls that place home, to drift no more.

Farewell

Farewell my co-workers and friends,
your laughter and joy I'll cherish,
never letting them come to an end.
We never looked at one another
thinking who was going to be the best.
As employers and employees we managed
to get the work done,
determined to be number one.
Our problems we faced through daily grace,
fast-moving yet always at a steady pace.
I'm remembering the day I walked through the door.
I was a whole new person waiting to explore.
Now it's time for me to say good-bye –
I'll miss you all – farewell.

Final Marks

I want these marks!
I believe I can achieve them.
It is a challenge every moment,
yes the pressure is on for that final mark.
Anxiety sets in; I try not to think so hard.
A time limit is set,
I break into a sweat
wondering how to cope with it all.
I look at the material placed in front of me.
The clock is nearing its last second
Now it's up to me to see it to the end,
to achieve those final marks.

For The Love of Me

For the love of me I was blind,
searching always for my Valentine.
I could not see the beauty within me,
yet I felt the warmth of being single and free.
For the love of me I feel no more pain,
only to realize that I have so much to gain.
Writing down the obstacles to overcome,
proving to myself that I am number one.
For the love of me I let go of stress;
meditation and yoga, my mind at rest.
The beauty within me I'd held all along,
as a single person I'm feeling quite strong.
For the love of me on Valentine's Day
Flowers, chocolates, a card on the way –
happy to be single and free,
this special card is for the love of me.

Friendship Rose

You gave to me a friendship rose;
a man like you I must get to know.
With the rose in your hand
you asked me to dance.
A breathtaking moment, the friendship enhanced.
I'll place your rose on my fireplace mantel,
your friendship is sincere, it's one I can handle.
The rose, to our surprise, brought joy to our hearts.
From the moment we met
we will never part.

Gopher's Hole

The gopher awakes furiously annoyed
To find me asleep in his hole.
"Get out!" he hollers. "This is my hole."
"Mr. Gopher please help me – I have nowhere to go."
His little ears listened,
allowing me to put my mind at ease.
Then he spoke: "Do you not realize
that you're the only *you* you have to please?
Listening to you change your mind several times.
Face it," the gopher said,
"you'll never have a satisfied mind."
My mind explodes with anger knowing he was right.
It was up to me to make everything all right.
The gopher says, "So you are feeling strong?"
"No, I'm wondering where I went wrong."
"No one said it was going to be easy."
The gopher proclaims, "You must listen to me.
I'll tell you what to do to ease your pain.
You must broaden your horizons,
learn to feel better about yourself,
let go of the stress – it will improve your health."
Nudging me out of his hole, he said,
"Go now, before you grow old,
take the lesson I've taught you.
Don't look back. Learn about the new you.
And by the way, stay out of my gopher hole."

Guardian Angel

I cannot bear the loneliness of being single,
partying all night till the crack of dawn,
not knowing when I would be returning home,
I'm so afraid, I'm all alone.

People say they care and want to reach out
and that they will be there.
They told me to keep an eye out
for the guardian angel –
she has wings, she'll follow you everywhere.

Sleepless nights I spent awake, waiting for the dawn,
hoping there would be another party going on.
Who was I? I was not me.
I'm so afraid, I'm all alone.

She only wanted to help me,
watching over me as I cried myself to sleep.
She claimed the strength and courage
will come from within.
I'm so afraid, I'm all alone.

At the darkest part of the night
a bright light shone through my bedroom window.
I could see her halo.
I'm so afraid, I'm all alone.

I could see her spreading her wings.
I arose from my bed
wiping the tears from my eyes.
You'll never be afraid, you'll never be alone.
I am your guardian angel,
I will always be your steppingstone.

Gossip Amongst Us

They walk through office corridors,
eyes focused on fellow workers,
ears open, waiting to hear scandalous gossip.
Employees confide in you
to keep what they are about to reveal, anonymous.
Sworn to secrecy not to repeat what they have mentioned,
the whole office is now in turmoil.
Embarrassed to come forward, showing no remorse,
they go into hiding, hoping the episode will clear.
It's too late. Immediate action has been taken.
Scared forever, they search for work,
sacrificing their own dignity
they claim to have learned a valuable lesson.
Spreading gossip amongst us has destroyed their self-worth.
Was it worth it? Did you enjoy it?
Did your heart not tell you enough was enough?
The choice is yours now – rid yourself of
the ungrateful crime you have committed.
Never spread gossip amongst us.

Gypsy

Gypsy I may be,
kind hearted, warm,
full of generosity.
Reaching out to everyone
my heart tells me
I need to be number one.
I travelled the countryside
far and beyond
trying to get in touch
with myself
and where I belong.
I have no real home
to call my own.
Forever happy, with the urge to roam;
searching for the answers
from signs above,
while I wander freely
across the land.

Hurts

"Are you starving yourself over me?
I'm not worth it,
I'm just a painful memory.
Look how thin you are.
Will you ever forgive me?
I can see you want to
get on with your life.
Let me help you to make everything all right.
There is a good shrink in town."
She was totally shocked and astounded.
Her worn-down body, teary blue eyes,
standing hopelessly listening to a pack of lies.
"I'm stronger than you think.
Could it be
that you need a shrink?"
Gathering her hurt memories,
she put them in the delete file.
Realizing that she was okay;
that he was the one in total denial.
Allowing herself time to heal,
she woke up to new kind of love –
one that gave her strength,
courage and the wisdom to heal.

I Will

I will let the past be my teacher
I will learn to accept what I cannot change
I will carry no burden that the past holds on me
I will love, I will make choices
I will let go of my anger
I will not judge myself
I will rise above any obstacles
that prevent me from going ahead.
I will let each day count as if it were my last
I will dry the tears that I have once wept
I will not journey into the past
I will gain knowledge through life experiences
that challenge me to carry on.
I will never give up on the lesson I have been taught.
I will love, I will make choices.
I will love every one that touches my heart.
I will let the future be my leader.

Inspiration

When you think of the career you have chosen
the inspiration to succeed lies within.
You will go through countless moments
wondering if the choices you made are the right ones.
You're excited and thrilled; you will define
all possibilities but you will
say to yourself, this is the path
I have been longing for.
The career you have chosen keeps your mind afloat.
You will be dealing with the young and old
working your way into their hearts.
There will be lots of homework,
study time must be accounted for,
setting your personal life aside to achieve your goals.
But a good factor is you are not alone –
you have family and friends
that want to see you succeed.
Believing in all the possibilities of the career you have chosen,
it's up to you to see it through.
You're strong-willed, good-natured,
your love for people throughout your life has made you gifted.
Knowing you and the career you have chosen,
you have the inspiration to see it through.

Lights

The amber light comes on.
Walking slowly to the curb
mind races, heart is pounding,
the thought of heading for home.

Red light, suddenly I stop.
Memory flashback of a family
torn between love and anger.
Would they, will they accept me back?
Still I must head for home.

Green light, I step off the curb,
pacing myself as I walk across the street.
The sun glares into my eyes,
vision of my family
waiting on the other side.
Am I finally going home?

All lights trigger go, stop and proceed with caution.
Go ahead – love thy family.
Try not to be too judgmental.
Stop! Stop procrastinating,
proceed with caution.
Feel the love that's hidden deep within your heart.
Now let's go home.

Looking Over My Shoulder

I feel you looking over my shoulder,
watching every move I make,
listening to every sound.
My heart grows colder, my temper flares,
watching you tiptoe around.
You don't notice me, but I noticed you
eavesdropping, hoping to hear something new.
I received a call,
shocked to notice that you were not on the ball.
Whispering as I spoke,
I realized I was not alone.
I was very annoyed.
Confronting was a tough call
but from that moment on,
my privacy you kept with great respect,
with no qualms or regret.

Moving

Scattered boxes all over the floor,
the doorbell rings, I open the door.
I haven't much time to sit and chatter,
you'll have to hurry.
Tell me, what's the matter?
I'm in a rush soon to be on my way,
don't you know it's my moving day?
I look at the time, it keeps ticking on.
Sorry, my friend, I cannot sit for long.
I look out the window – my truck is here.
Come now, my friend, wipe away those tears.
I'll be back to see you in a couple of years.
The boxes are loaded onto the truck.
Goodbye, my friend,
and the best of luck.

My Child

From the moment I found out that I was pregnant
I carried you, nine months long,
excited and anxious, awaiting the day of your birth.
When I saw you, held you for the first time,
wrapped in a warm blanket, bonnet on your head,
you were my bundle of joy, my child.
Your eyes so pure, fingers held tightly to mine,
we bonded forever.
When back to the nursery you went
I held back the tears, yet knew I needed my rest
and you too needed yours.
I nearly dozed off; the phone rang;
kinfolk's calling from away.
They wanted to meet you, my child,
dressed in the finest store-bought clothes.
You whimpered and fussed but oh how adorable always.
When kinfolk arrived you were sound asleep in my arms.
Nudging to see if you would wake,
you opened your eyes for a brief moment
but sleepy time fell upon you.
My child you rest, you will need your strength
to make the journey home.
I'm overwhelmed with the joy of taking you home.
The kinfolk assured me I have a mother's instinct
passed on through generations.
Knowing they are right, my mind is at ease.
My bundle of joy, my child, let's go home.

Mysterious Man

I'm sitting staring at the computer screen,
waiting for the mysterious man
whom I have not met or seen,
wanting to believe he was out there somewhere.
The full moon was out,
romance was in the air.
Online searching from A to Z,
startled by his appearance,
the mysterious man sent a message to me.
Could it be fate, was destiny on our side?
Vision of his character, the passion,
fighting feelings I could not hide.
He revealed his identity, taking me by surprise,
still the mysterious man I did not recognize.
Replying to his message, only to have faith,
I wanted him to know this mysterious woman
could very well be his mate.

No Diploma

She weeps, her blue eyes reddened by tears she had shed.
The door closes to her recent job.
Her little white lie, held deep inside,
a lie about a diploma.

Pleading for mercy to hold onto her job,
an income to survive.
Working skills, living skills, do they not count?
Feeling deeply deprived.

Clouds darken – the outcome of her future.
Good spirits, highly motivated,
certainly not a quitter,
she will seek to do what it takes.

Her trust in all humankind
at its lowest ebb,
lead her not into temptation.
A sacrifice of dignity
forced to depend on the system
her blue eyes still weep.

Diploma

Astounded by the news she had received
With her hearing slightly off she replayed her voicemail.
She wanted to believe that this was the call
she'd been longing for.
A few years had passed, struggling for success.
She was determined not to be a quitter.
Every day attending classes
hearing words of wisdom from her teacher.
How those words inspired her.
She did not know how to accept the fact
that she herself was the one
who put forth the effort,
her brain did not rest.
The message stated:
*Congratulations, your big brown envelope
is on its way.*
That meant only one thing –
it was my diploma.
Now for the first time in my life
I can accept the fact that I am a graduate.

Penny Dive

Pennies are worth their weight in gold
having been saved by the young and old.
Rolled up in the Hilroy paper
squirrelled away for many years later.
Struggling to survive, the pennies well saved,
it was time to do a copper dive;
difficult times can't last forever.
The penny dive carried us through stormy weather.
The brown paper bags were our disguise,
and kept a person from seeing what lay inside.
Sacrificing our dignity we still had our pride.
With the bank soon to open looking all around;
people of all ages firmly stood their ground.
The pennies like gold to the teller we give
Feeling so happy with paper money to live.
Leaving the bank I've still got my pride,
counting my blessings, my pennies helped me survive.

Proposal In The Snow

We pranced through the fresh white snow;
temperature falling to twenty below.
The coldness I did not feel,
bundled so warmly with you by my side;
I felt a love that was real.
Stumbling over my feet,
landing face-first in the snow.
Smiling, looking up at you with such a glow.
Down on your knees you fell
proposing to me.
It was like a snow angel had cast a spell.
The diamond ring you placed on my hand,
followed by a gold wedding band,
we continued to prance through fresh white snow.
How we touched each other's heart
Cherishing that moment, vowing never to let go.

Poets Work

I print,
I write,
I scribble,
I scratch,
searching for words
that rhyme and match.
Fictional characters come alive.
Each poem that I write –
they all survive.
With my head just a-spinning
I search of a beginning,
I scribble and scratch
In hopes of an ending.
Hard at work, the critics critique.
The poems that I've written
Have a deadline to meet.
Onto the computer
To be printed as so.
Sent to a publisher
for the green light to go.
Patience is a virtue;
as an author you wait,
expecting the unknown –
a poem is poem.

Relationship Hurdles

I await the day you will change
heart-breaking memories
to ease your pain.
Pouring down rain, weather still the same.
How can I mend your broken heart?
Hurricane winds blowing ashore
putting you on a pedestal
to search for love, to explore.
How can I mend your broken heart?
As the sun rises above the sea,
we look on the bright side,
our minds at ease.
Pouring down rain, hurricane winds,
relationship hurdles soon to end.
Now I can mend your broken heart.

Separate Vacations

It was not in the cards to meet you right away.
Taking separate vacations
so my heart doesn't stray.
Although we have never met, listening to my heart,
the Powerful One gave his blessing
For a fresh new start.
You called me on the telephone just to say hello.
Rushing to pack my suitcase
I had to let you go.
The Powerful One reached for my cell phone.
It's time for you to be alone.
Determined to do as He proclaimed,
my heart was aching, I could not bear the pain
togetherness with you was not meant to be.
The desire to be loved was up to me.
Opening my eyes to discover what's real –
that was the person I needed to feel.
Separate vacations I came to accept:
no self-doubt or any regrets.

Shadow of Fear

Overcoming the shadow of fear,
remembering the time
my body would tremble
when people were near.
Trying to walk safely down the city streets,
holding my head up high
greeting the people I meet.
Danger was all around,
I was too scared
to even utter a sound.
I see no evil, I fear no evil
side by side I walk with other people.
Now with a peaceful mind
my trembling body rids itself of the pain,
casting out the emotions of fear.
A courageous effort it took to overcome
the shadow of fear.

Shadow

Walking barefoot along the ocean shore
hearing the wave
slapping against the wharf,
it sounded like subliminal music.
Edging my way into the cold ocean
I stood knee deep, swirling my hands to and fro
gazing into the water
I caught a glimpse of my own shadow.
I moved, it moved, would it speak if I spoke?
Curiosity got the best of me,
with such a vivid imagination
I hollered, "Destiny awaits me."
I did not get fooled by this
For I believe in myself
without a doubt, we are inseparable.

Shelter

Don't pass on by as if I were a stranger.
I mean you no harm;
just to keep you safe
and out of danger.
Peace of mind will help you heal.
We will guide you to a life
rich and real.
You will be safe away from danger.
We're ready to deal
with your frustration and anger.
I have many rooms, food galore,
There's always room for just one more.
Required of you –
a few daily chores.
The shelter will help you
a new life to explore.
I will assign you a legal advisor
in hopes that you'll become wiser.
Now take my hand,
as I walk you inside,
the shelter is safe,
there you can hide.

Speaking Out

I looked for work. Companies would not hire me.
Education they say is a major priority.
I speak out: "Then you educate me!
Set my mind at ease."
Returning to school at a golden age,
hoping to get a decent grade.
A, B, C, the saviour of D,
was the grading mark
in the year of seventy-three.
Now a mark of four-fifty I recollect,
before I was able to graduate.
Study hard they say,
a diploma will be waiting for you
on that final day.
With the age that I am
can you not give me an easy exam?
A grade-twelve diploma
would mean the world to me.
Work is my major priority,
on the job training I could accept.
There I could show a hard-working person
who has already been a graduate.

Spirits of the Unknown

Spirits of the unknown casting a spell –
married but have the urge to roam.
Why, pray tell?
Spirits of the unknown, the fragrance and the passion.
Only to feel the desire to deceive,
no special occasion, no gifts to receive,
only to live in a world of make-believe.
Spirits of the unknown reminding you,
how unhappy you are at home.
The spouse who loves you
hopes in their heart you'll be returning home.
Spirits of the unknown
cannot justify your behaviour.
Were not the vows to become one
signed on a legal paper?
Hang on to the love that is real,
spirits of the unknown.

Story

Am I just a story for you to write?
You could blink your eyes to make-believe.
Be-mine roses, champagne glasses,
still I'm just a story
a magical illusion, creating that special someone
who will touch your heart and soul.
Pictures, words, we all seem so focused on,
fictional, non-fictional characters
we all try to be.
Overrated match-making, playing detective
to solve the mystery.
When will the story end?

Talk To Me

Words cannot describe the strength
or weakness that one feels.
Talk to me – I can help.
Taunting memories from the past
still linger in your mind.
Talk to me from the heart that is real,
don't let silence fill the air.
There's strength within you –
talk to me, I can help you.
Let me bring out the weakness
you hold on to.
You can run but you cannot hide.
Believe in me, confide in me,
let me guide you through.
Talk to me from the heart that is real.

The Bottle

When I hit the bottle I can't get out.
Don't make excuses for me,
this is my doubt.
Don't drag me to an AA meeting –
when I am ready I will walk on my own.
I can fight the times I reach for the bottle
but what I cannot fight is what I have lost.
I scrounge on the ground picking up every cent I can find;
I need that bottle, I am losing my mind.
I could hide from here to eternity
but when I look in the mirror
this is not the person I choose to be.
Bottle, let it be known
you can be my friend
you can be my enemy
but it's me who's in charge of the bottle.

The Cookie Jar

His trembling hands reached for the cookie jar –
how he wanted that mustang car.
Inside the cookie jar was our retirement wealth.
How could he be so cruel to think of himself?
A man and his toys will never part
I'm sure he loves me with all his heart.
He took the money, out the door he ran
looking back to say, "I know you will understand."
With my heart so confused,
trying to get through to him.
The addiction to his toys, where does one begin?
He drove into the driveway
in his old run-down car.
There was no sign of the mustang so far.
It is true a man and his toys will never part,
yet at that moment he had a change of heart,
the retirement wealth put back in the jar.
Not a word mentioned about the mustang car.
A man and his toys will never part;
I'm sure he loves me with all his heart.

The Gambling Man

He couldn't control his urge to gamble
despite his life, his work, in shambles.
The sound of the slot machine had him cursing
because the money was not dispersing.
The crowd gathers around the blackjack table.
His mind not at ease, nor his hand stable
reaching out for someone to be his saviour
he couldn't overcome his compulsive behaviour.
He upped his wager –
slot machine, blackjack –
as he put his earnings on the table
his life became completely unstable.

The Healing House

The uncertainty of your addiction
causes you so much grief and friction.
I will always be there though not as a spouse
to lead you into the healing house.
You fought with me all the way,
pleading not to make you stay.
You cried with mixed emotion;
within four walls you felt so doomed.
Your trembling soul could not enter the room,
you were not ready to confess your sins.
A voice from beyond spoke: "Let's begin."
You felt a hand touch your shoulder,
nudging you to get closer.
Your addiction was driving you insane,
admitting to yourself you were to blame.
It took several weeks of devotion,
struggling through all mental emotions.
With good instructors by your side
you were able to get over your foolish pride.
Highly praised for admitting your addictions
yet still limited by some restrictions
the healing house gave you great courage –
the wisdom never to get discouraged.

The Moral of the Old Truck

Driving down a country road
the poor old truck was ready to quit.
It sputtered and knocked,
giving the impression
that it could not be fixed.
Coasting downhill close to home,
shifting gears so as not to stall,
it had to prove it was capable of surviving.
I took the truck to a mechanic
who specialized in old trucks.
He could tell the truck was antique
but he stated, "We all age at
some point in our life."
With a few adjustments to the body
and some helpful instructions,
this old truck will make it.

The Letter

The postman hands me a letter
and continues down the corridor.
I hold the letter in my trembling hand,
not knowing who sent it or what the letter holds.
Opening the letter there's still no name. Who is this person?
Were they out to play head games?
There must be some mistake. This letter is not for me.
I don't recall knowing anyone
who would write me a letter.
Behind the locked security doors,
still holding the letter in my hand,
I cried out, "Help me to understand!"
The person who wrote the letter
must surely have been missed.
I must read on, maybe I can help
about where they belong.
Faced with memory loss,
wanting so much to understand
what the letter was about.
The following day the postman returns.
"Here, please take this letter. Send it back
to the one who sent it."
He expressed his concerns:
"May I help you to understand this letter?"
It turned out the letter was
from a dear friend
suffering from dementia.
She just wanted to know if I was still her friend.

The Soldiers

Put yourself in the soldiers' shoes
waiting for the moment to come back home,
wondering each day, each breath they take
when this terrible war will end.

They sacrifice all achievement to help other countries.
Put yourself in their shoes,
those who have lost their lives
and those who are still at war.

Remember, when the war begins,
remember how we honour them.
Pray that every day they toil
they will return to home soil.
Put yourself in the soldiers' shoes.

The Stove Is The Heart

The stove is the heart that makes the elements glow.
It's the only thing that should take control;
temperature rises, friction among the elements grows,
severely scorched, no reasoning in sight
To refuel the love torch.
Medium heat gets us elements to a slight turning point.
The spark is there, will it ignite?
The low heat of the elements
is slow passion, our love revived.
The simmering of the elements show
The greatest strength of all.
Now replenished in love,
we come to realize that the stove is the heart
and it's the only thing that should take control.

The Thought

I'm frantic, the piggy bank is empty.
Two dollars and sixty-seven cents to my name
with Christmas coming and gifts to buy
my mind is exploding, I feel I am going insane.

I could run and hide but that means
I would miss out on Christmas.
It is such a joyous time of giving and receiving
I know my family would still love me
even if I couldn't afford to buy them gifts.

I must put my thinking cap on!
I am not totally broke after all; I still have
two dollars and sixty-seven cents.
I went into the village keeping my spirits up,
scuffing my boots through the fresh white snow
I was in search of a low-priced store.

At last right before my eyes in huge big letters:
Dollar Store "Come in – we're open."
In I walk with my two dollars and sixty-seven cents
holding it tightly in the palm of my hand.
Finally a brain wave:
the art paper, the pencil crayons –
the spirit of Christmas was back.
Homemade cards are
what my family will receive.
In those cards will be a chore
That I will do for them
For in my heart it's the thought
behind the gift that means the most.

The Teacher's Words

If you come to school, I will teach,
my time and yours both valuable,
a diploma you will earn;
we must work together to achieve this goal.
I will give what I know for you to meet your need.
With enthusiasm and motivation
you can and will succeed.
The curriculum that I teach
will generate self-worth,
for knowledge you will yearn.
So if you come to school
I will teach and you will learn.

The Will

It's no joke I'm on my way out;
no papers are signed I haven't much time.
I'll pull myself together I'm sure without a doubt.
The doctor calls the family in
breaking the news the tears begin.
"She hasn't much time," he says in a soft voice.
"Her dying wishes must be her choice."
With tears in my eyes I speak out –
"My dear family not to worry, my Will is made out."
They look at each other in total despair.
Who will be the next in line as the family heir?
Giving the family time to heal their wounds,
the doctor and I left the room.
Left alone they fought out loud
I was not impressed nor too proud.
The Will consisted of who gets what,
neither great fortune nor big bucks.
"Family," I say, "kneel down to pray.
God is coming soon to take me away."
Scolding them one by one my life will soon be over –
yours has just begun.
They bowed their heads in sorrow and shame;
we know our life without you will never be the same.
God has given me some extra time
To sign the papers on the dotted line.
I assure my family you'll do just fine,
now I will lay myself to rest with a satisfied mind.

Think Twice

When you cloud your thoughts to the person who has mistreated
you
you wake up feeling alone, wondering if they're ever going to
change.
Your mind is in overdrive, it's like asking a zebra to remove its
stripes.
You can try many a time to make an effort but
it's not them who has to change –
it's yourself.

If you want to make sacrifices and accept that he will not change,
take a deep breath, let your mind rest at ease.
Continue with the strength and courage
that kept you going throughout the relationship,
be strong about the choices you have made.

Don't stay with him if you feel you have to;
cater to all his whims and wishes.
Not only will he suffer but you as well
if you cannot see the good in one another.
Stop wasting your life and his.
There will come a time when you will both realize
that it's time to wake up.

Starting over is not easy but it's time to
look beyond the misery that held you back.
Set forth to a new life; take a moment to consider the conse-
quences;
start making some right choices – stay or go.
The answer to it all lies beneath the heart that has been broken.
Save his life as well yours – think twice before staying.

Ties To Work

What we have learned throughout life –
our skills, our knowledge – no longer counts.
With society forever changing
to learn we must study
through knowledge we gain experience.
Success we thrive on;
a will to succeed,
assessments and evaluation
reading, documentations, money, math.
Each of us challenged at our own level.
Recognition of our achievement
is gratitude, appreciation.
Through ties to work and team spirit
we further develop our abilities,
the inspiration to meet our goals
at last complete.

To Nurture a Spouse

To go the distance, to nurture a spouse –
you've got to feel the inspiration
from within your heart,
Believing anything is possible.
They may come upon illness;
you will feel their aches and pains.
You will nurture them through to recovery
not asking or wanting anything in return.
It could be that your spouse
longs for a career change
yet is timid to take that chance,
wondering if his significant other
will stand behind him.
With this in mind, decision and choices
have to be made.
The decision of the outcome and income
all depends on life's reality.
Your choice to guide him through
will ease his mind.
It may require you to set aside the routine
you have become accustomed to.
When all is said and done, the gratitude
of nurturing him toward something he has been longing for
will be in his heart forever, as well as yours.
You will feel rewarded knowing that you have gone the distance.

Train Thirteen

He shovelled coal into the engine of the train
intrigued by scurrying passengers.
The drawn-out look, soot around his eyes.
he always managed to keep a smile on his face
until one day a letter was posted on the train door.
Train thirteen must be terminated; its service is no longer required
due to a decrease in our financial status.
He took the letter and shoved it in his pocket,
his mind racing a mile a minute.
The whistle blows, jet-black smoke pours from the engine
then, without notice, he pulls the cord to put on the brakes.
Passengers are startled and even more shook up
when he reads the letter.
They want their voices to be heard;
a petition was written up and signed by all.
It stated: *The commute to the big city saves us time and fuel;*
ticket prices are reasonable;
devastated if the train operator/engineer
is forced into retirement.
It was a tense situation for both parties at hand
waiting the verdict for train thirteen.
At last the letter was posted.
When the reply came,
with the drawn-out look, soot around his eyes,
could he bear to read it? Then the smile that passengers had seen
many times set their mind at ease.
The train thirteen will not derail.

Utmost Attention

Sitting all alone in a honky-tonk mansion,
trying to get your utmost attention.
Empty rooms that once were filled,
dust on the old guitar,
cobwebs on the curtains that frayed,
Each day goes by, thinking
you will be returning home.
The music, the guitar, your urge to roam.
I tried to get your utmost attention.
Playing second fiddle to an old guitar I dare to mention.
Now the honky-tonk mansion was put up for sale.
Still dust on the old guitar,
still cobwebs on the curtain that frayed.
I had to see you one more time,
before I signed on the dotted line.
Needing your utmost attention
to assure you that I would be fine –
your presence I felt.

Whiskey Joe

Through the corridors of the county jail
Whiskey Joe paces the floors, biding his time
until he is released.
Feeble-minded, he was unaware of his actions,
remembering in small detail
about the evil spirit of whiskey.
He cursed the day it touched his lips.
Lock down was in effect;
soon the pastor would be around
to recite the evening prayer.
He could never imagine listening to someone so spiritual.
His patience was running on a short circuit.
He used broken English to speak:
"You all know me as Whiskey Joe."
There was a moment of silence.
It was time for him to repent his sins.
"You all know that I drank the evil spirits of whiskey.
I stumbled and I fell, committing crimes
that I regret."

The pastor walked up to my cell:
"Well spoken, my lad."
He held my hand through the cell bars
as he recited the evening prayer.
The day finally came – he was being released.
He nodded his head with the utmost gratitude
as he walked through the corridors for the last time.
The pastor, the inmates,
including the guards,
bid farewell to the man they knew
as Whiskey Joe.

Whatcha Doing, Girl?

Whatcha doing out there all alone, girl?
Shall we give this dance a whirl?
Captivated by his charm, only to feel inspired.
On the other hand feeling,
like a spontaneous wild fire,
jiving to the beat of the band,
holding on to his manly hands.
Whatcha doing, girl, out all alone?
Is there a chance a man like me
can take you on home?
I could not bear to reply; he took me by surprise.
The romance I yearned the desire to have,
Was happening right before my eyes.
Whatcha doing, guy, out here all alone
captivated by my flirtatious ways?
On the other hand,
would it be out of character to let my heart sway?
He could not bear to reply,
still yearning to take me home.
Hey girl! Hey guy! Whatcha going to do now?
Dance to the beat of that crazy love spell?
The companionship, the passion,
of getting to know one another
we dare to enhance – it's our life to discover.

Work Brains Off

I grab a coffee and a bagel-to-go.
Traffic moving slowly, oh so slow,
let your brain relax;
go with the flow.
Stepping inside my office
my brain tells me so –
I've totally lost it.
The phones are ringing!
There's a crisis on the other end.
Will the day ever end?
Immune system is totally run down.
Must get it together
Or be six feet underground.
Warning signs from the angels above.
Listen to us, feel our love.
Work-brain off, I will obey
the angels' words and what they say.
I grab a coffee, a bagel-to-go,
heading home traffic moving oh so slow.
Work-brain off, I have learned to let go.

You My Dear Are The One

Knowing how to connect, how to bond,
takes a special someone.
You've taught me to love again,
never to feel incapable or to doubt
the true meaning of love.
You, my dear, are the one.

A foundation of love
does not happen overnight.
To have you as my friend
my companion, and most of all my love.
You, my dear, are the one.

My friend, the richness of one's heart
sees you through difficult times
that may arise,
my companion, side-by-side.
We will travel life as a journey, our destiny entwined.
You, my dear, are the one.

My love, as we exchange
our hearts and souls,
our sacred vows from this day on,
by the power of love we bonded as one.
You, my dear, are the one.

A Friendship Letter

'Tis the letter we wrote
from East Coast to West Coast.
'Tis not a contest,
of who could write the most.
'Tis the test of writing by hand.
'Tis something people don't understand.
'Tis a letter that comes
from the heart.
'Tis our friendship we'll never part.
'Tis no computer
can stand in the way.
'Tis a hand-written letter –
must be written today.

Come Back To Me

From the shores of New Brunswick
to the shores of Newfoundland
there's not a day goes by,
without wishing you were mine.
We seem to be so much in love
but with the ocean between us, we drift apart.

Come back to me, my love,
let us share our golden years.
Set sail on the boat from Newfoundland
for I will be waiting on the other side.
I know our hearts are waiting
to share those golden years.
Lord give me the strength to hold on. Set sail, my love.

I feel the bond between us grow
for you, my love, you are the one.
Set sail across the ocean,
come home to me.
This is where you belong
Our golden years are waiting.

Communication

Long ago, communication with our
kinfolk and friends felt so real.
You'd see them coming up the driveway,
toss another teabag in the tea kettle,
welcome hugs and a peck on the cheek,
as they all gathered around the kitchen table
communicating with each other
about their life events.
Body language and the tone of one's voice
depending on the situation was quite remarkable.
We knew and understood one another;
facial expressions were used when words
could not describe how one felt.
In the midst of long ago
communicating amongst kinfolk and family felt so real.
It was a bond we shared to become whole;
this is what communication is all about.

Cold Turkey

She is weak but she wants to be strong.
She knows somehow life must go on.
She wants so badly to move along
and kick the habit that's done her wrong.
She knows deep down, she wants to quit
yet the craving hits her every day.
It's tough to make it go away.
Hoping every morning that this is the day
when the cigarette craving will go away.
It's been a week since she had a puff –
God help her now it's really tough.
This nicotine addiction is really severe
she'll hang in, she'll persevere,
her breath comes easier every day.
The garbage in her lungs is clearing away.
Another week without the weed –
she's on her way, she's done her deed.
No more weakness, she's feeling quite strong.
She's kicked the habit that's done her wrong.

Lone Wolf

In the change of season
The lone wolf stands alone,
his log cabin nestled among the tall pine trees.
He strolls through the forest
listening to the sound of the falling leaves.
The lone wolf stands alone.
He cries for the ocean and lakes.
Loves and lives nature
with every breath that he takes.
Look deeply into his eyes,
they will take you by surprise.
His quest for love, his romance
you will take the chance.
The lone wolf no longer alone.

CPSIA information can be obtained
at www.ICGtesting.com
Printed in the USA
LVOW01s1104150417
530793LV00008B/16/P

9 781460 270127